Sing Nowell

34 favourite carols to sing and play

Arranged by **Timothy Roberts** and **Jan Betts**

MUSIC AND CD EDITION

A&C Black • London

Contents

Second edition 2008
A&C Black Publishers Ltd
38 Soho Square, London W1D 3HB
© 2008, 1989 A&C Black Publishers Ltd
Cover illustration © 2008 Leslie Saddington
Inside illustrations © 2008 Tatiana Demidova

ISBN 978-1-4081-0424-8

BOOK:
Music set by Jeanne Roberts
Design by Tatiana Demidova
Compiled by Sheena Roberts
Edited by Sheena Roberts, Uchenna Ngwe and Lucy Mitchell

CD:
Songs performed by Kaz Simmons
Backing tracks arranged by David Smith
Engineered by Matthew Moore
© 2008 A&C Black Publishers Ltd

This book has been produced using paper that is made from wood grown in managed, sustainable forests. It is natural, renewable and recyclable. The logging and manufacturing processes conform to the environmental regulations of the country of origin.

Printed by Halstan Printing Group, Amersham, Buckinghamshire.

About the Arrangements

Acknowledgements

Throughout this collection the aim has been to preserve the familiar harmonies to these well-known carols within very simple arrangements. Pianists of around grade three standard should find pleasure in playing the piano accompaniments, which may be easily filled out by the more skilled player.

In all but one of the carols, the guitar chords (which may also be used by autoharps or electronic keyboards) are compatible with the piano harmonies. (In the chorus of **Ding dong merrily on high**, the guitar and piano harmonies part company; a simpler progression of chords is given to the guitar.) Sometimes a simpler alternative chord is shown (eg F/Dm7): this will not exactly match the piano harmony but will be easier for the guitar to play. Capo chords are given in brackets in a number of the carols. The capo chords may be used *with* the capo as simpler alternatives, or *without* the capo to lower the pitch of the singing when only the guitar is accompanying.

Simple parts for percussion or other instruments are provided throughout. More than half of the arrangements also provide parts for second voices or more advanced instrumentalists. Although recorders, tuned and untuned percussion have been borne in mind particularly, the part-writing will suit a wider range of instruments, and it is often left to the teacher to decide on the instrumentation. When an instrument is thought specially suitable, this has been stated. For instance, the three-note part which chases the melody line through **The holly and the ivy** is given to tuned percussion. On the other hand, if a recorder part is outside the range of the treble this is also stated.

When a part is given in letter names rather than staff notation, a stroke below the letter denotes the octave below, a stroke above denotes the octave above. For instance, C, is an octave lower than C which is an octave lower than C'. In parts which may be played by tuned percussion, a list of the notes is given in brackets at the beginning so that the teacher may see at a glance which will be required.

This new edition is accompanied by two CDs. A performance of the first verse of each carol is given, followed by a backing track which includes all of the verses. See the inside back cover for the track list.

Grateful acknowledgement is made to Oxford University Press for permission to use the following copyright items from the *Oxford Book of Carols* © 1928:

Little Jesus, sweetly sleep (*Rocking*) – melody collected by Martin Shaw.

On Christmas Night (*The Sussex Carol*) – melody collected by R. Vaughan Williams, words by Ursula Vaughan Williams.

Sing aloud on this day – words translated by John Parkinson.

Shepherds left their flocks (*Quem pastores*) – words by Imogen Holst.

Unto us a boy is born – words translated by Geoffrey Shaw.

Also, for **Nowell, sing Nowell** – words translated by John Rutter © Oxford University Press 1969.

O little town of Bethlehem – melody (*Forest Green*) collected and arranged by R. Vaughan Williams (1872–1958), from the **English Hymnal**, © 1906 Oxford University Press.

Every effort has been made to trace and acknowledge copyright owners. If any right has been omitted, the publishers offer their apologies and will rectify this in subsequent editions following notification.

All piano accompaniments (except that by Jan Betts to **Joseph dearest, Joseph mine**) are by Timothy Roberts. Guitar chords are by Jan Betts. Additional parts for second voices, instruments and percussion are by Jan Betts and Timothy Roberts.

A child this day is born

1 A child this day is born,
   A child of high renown,
   Most worthy of a sceptre,
   A sceptre and a crown.
      Nowell, Nowell, Nowell,
      Nowell sing all we may,
      Because the King of all kings
      Was born this blessèd day.

2 These tidings shepherds heard
   In field watching their fold,
   Were by an angel unto them
   That night revealed and told.
      Nowell, Nowell, Nowell…

3 To whom the angel spoke,
   Saying, 'Be not afraid:
   Be glad, poor simple shepherds,
   Why are you so dismayed?'
      Nowell, Nowell, Nowell…

4 'For lo! I bring you tidings
   Of gladness and of mirth,
   Which cometh to all people by
   This holy infant's birth.'
      Nowell, Nowell, Nowell…

Chorus

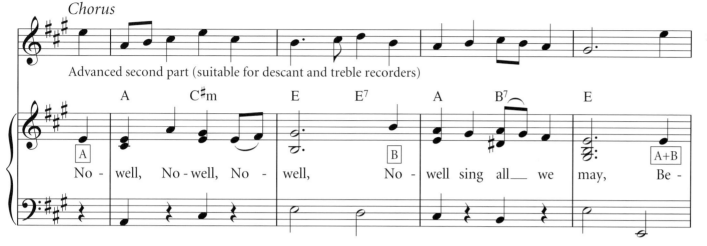

Advanced second part (suitable for descant and treble recorders)

A   C♯m   E   E⁷   A   B⁷   E

A

No - well, No - well, No - well,   No - well sing all___ we   may,   B

A+B

Be -

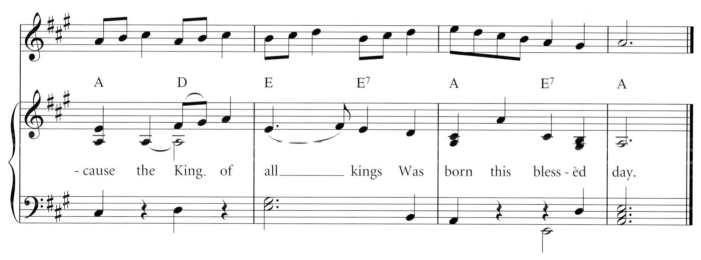

A   D   E   E⁷   A   E⁷   A

- cause   the   King_   of   all_____ kings   Was   born   this   bless - èd   day.

5 And as the angel told them,
   So to them did appear;
   They found the young child, Jesus Christ,
   With Mary his mother dear.
      Nowell, Nowell, Nowell…

Words and melody: traditional English, from Sandys'
'Christmas Carols' (1833)

The easy second part for instruments can be played during the chorus as well as the verse. The more advanced second part can be played by treble recorders during the verse as well as the chorus.

Tuned percussion
Play the easy second part, and/or the letter names of the guitar chords (A C♯ D E B).

Untuned percussion
Select a pair of contrasting instruments, eg triangle and woodblock, or bells and maracas. One instrument plays the rhythm of the melody in the section marked A, the other plays the melody rhythm through the section marked B. Both play together at A + B. Choose a different pair of instruments for the chorus.

Angels from the realms of glory

1 Angels from the realms of glory,
  Wing your flight o'er all the earth;
  Ye who sang creation's story
  Now proclaim Messiah's birth:
    Gloria in excelsis Deo,
    Gloria in excelsis Deo.

2 Shepherds in the field abiding,
  Watching o'er your flocks by night,
  God with man is now residing,
  Yonder shines the Infant Light:
    Gloria in excelsis Deo…

3 Sages, leave your contemplations;
  Brighter visions beam afar.
  Seek the great desire of nations;
  Ye have seen his natal star:
    Gloria in excelsis Deo…

Words: James Montgomery (1771–1854)
Melody: traditional French tune

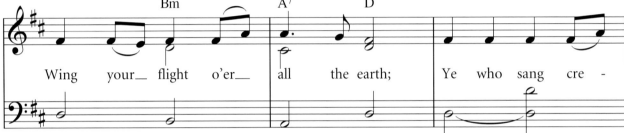

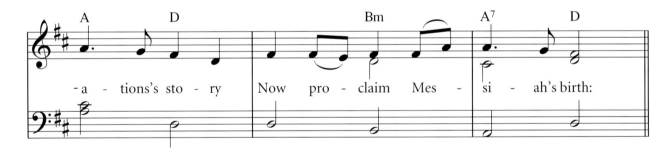

Easy tenor recorders or tuned percussion (D E G A D′)

Chorus

Away in a manger

1 Away in a manger
   no crib for a bed,
The little Lord Jesus
   laid down his sweet head.
The stars in the bright sky
   looked down where he lay,
The little Lord Jesus
   asleep on the hay.

2 The cattle are lowing,
   the baby awakes,
But little Lord Jesus
   no crying he makes.
I love thee, Lord Jesus;
   look down from the sky,
And stay by my side
   until morning is nigh.

3 Be near me, Lord Jesus;
   I ask thee to stay
Close by me for ever,
   and love me, I pray.
Bless all the dear children
   in thy tender care,
And fit us for heaven,
   to live with thee there.

Words: anon
Melody: W.J. Kirkpatrick (1838–1921)

Sing Nowell • © 2008 A&C Black Publishers Ltd

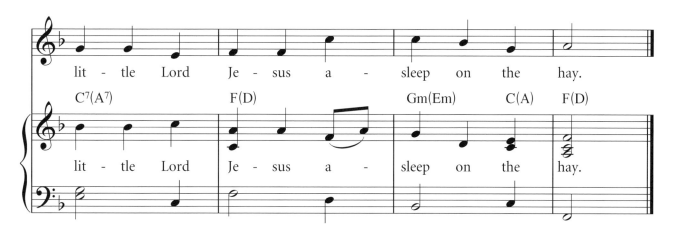

lit - tle Lord Je - sus a - sleep on the hay.

C⁷(A⁷)   F(D)   Gm(Em)   C(A)   F(D)

lit - tle Lord Je - sus a - sleep on the hay.

Tuned percussion (G A B C′ D′ E′ F′ / C D F G A)

Untuned percussion
Choose contrasting pairs of instruments to play rhythms A and B respectively. For example; tambour (with soft beater) and tambourine; or drum (soft beater) and bells; cymbal and maracas. Vary the combination in each verse.

As with gladness

1 As with gladness men of old
   Did the guiding star behold,
   As with joy they hailed its light
   Leading onward, beaming bright,
   So, most gracious God, may we
   Evermore be led to thee.

2 As with joyful steps they sped
   To that lowly manger-bed,
   There to bend the knee before
   Him whom heaven and earth adore,
   So may we with willing feet
   Ever seek thy mercy-seat.

3 As they offered gifts most rare
   At that manger rude and bare,
   So may we with holy joy,
   Pure and free from sin's alloy,
   All our costliest treasures bring,
   Christ, to thee our heavenly King.

Words: W.C. Dix (1837–98)
Melody: adapted from a chorale
by Konrad Kocher (1786–1872)

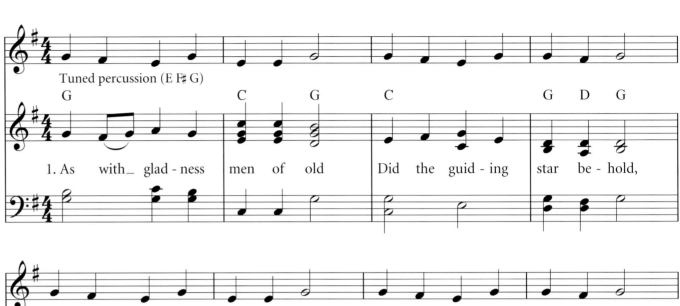

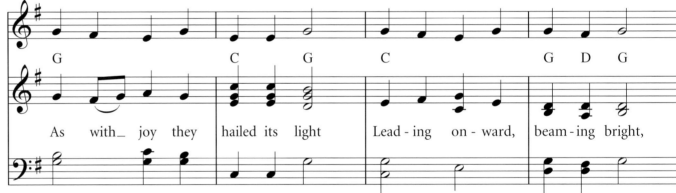

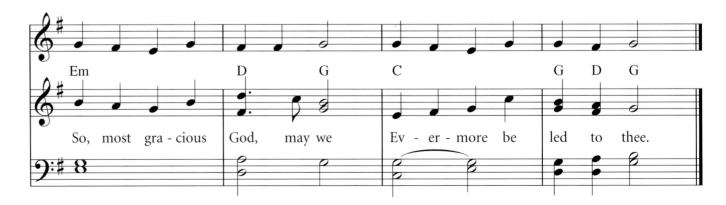

Child in the manger

1 Child in a manger,
Infant of Mary,
Outcast and stranger,
Lord of all!
Child who inherits
All our transgressions,
All our demerits
On him fall.

2 Once the most holy
Child of salvation,
Gently and lowly,
Lived below;
Now as our glorious
Mighty redeemer,
See him victorious
O'er each foe.

3 Prophets foretold him,
Infant of wonder;
Angels behold him
On his throne;
Worthy our Saviour
Of all their praises;
Happy for ever
Are his own.

Words: Mary Macdonald, translated by Lachlan Macbean
Melody: traditional Gaelic tune

Tambour (soft beater)

Deck the halls

1 Deck the halls with boughs of holly,
    Fa la la la la, la la la la,
'Tis the season to be jolly,
    Fa la la la la, la la la la.
Don we now our gay apparel,
    Fa la la, la la la, la la la,
Sing the ancient Yule-tide carol,
    Fa la la la la, la la la la.

2 See the blazing Yule before us,
    Fa la la la la, la la la la,
Strike the harp and join the chorus,
    Fa la la la la, la la la la.
Follow me in merry measure,
    Fa la la, la la la, la la la.
While I tell of Yule-tide treasure,
    Fa la la la la, la la la la.

3 Fast away the old year passes,
    Fa la la la la, la la la la,
Hail the new, you lads and lasses,
    Fa la la la la, la la la la
Sing we joyous all together,
    Fa la la, la la la, la la la,
Heedless of the wind and weather,
    Fa la la la la, la la la la.

Words: traditional English
Melody: 'Nos Galan', traditional Welsh carol

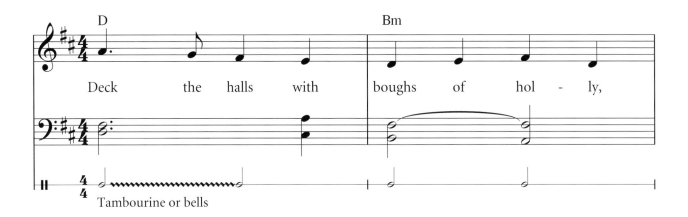

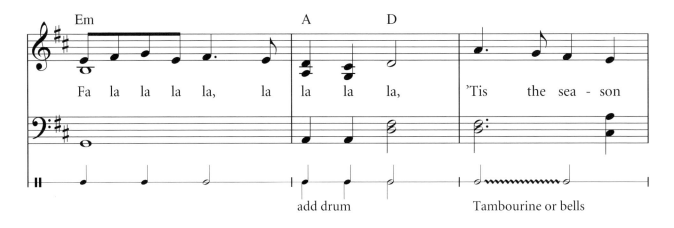

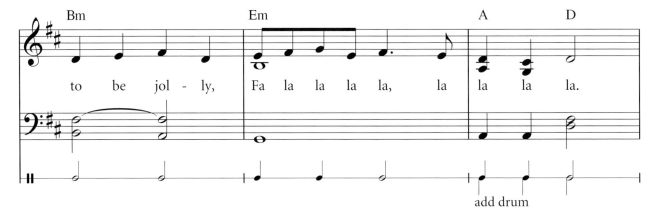

• © 2008 A&C Black Publishers Ltd

Don we now our gay ap-pa-rel, Fa la la, la la la, la la la,

Tambourine or bells

add drum

Sing the an-cient Yule-tide ca-rol, Fa la la la la, la la la la.

Tambourine or bells

add drum

Easy recorders or tuned percussion (A B D' E' A')

(perc.)

(rec.)

Ding dong merrily on high

1 Ding dong merrily on high!
   In heav'n the bells are ringing.
   Ding dong verily the sky
   Is riv'n with angels singing:
       Gloria, hosanna in excelsis!
       Gloria, hosanna in excelsis!

2 E'en so here below, below
   Let steeple bells be swungen.
   And io, io, io
   By priest and people sungen;
       Gloria, hosanna in excelsis!
       Gloria, hosanna in excelsis!

3 Pray you, dutifully prime
   Your matin chime, ye ringers;
   May you beautifully rime
   Your evetime song, ye singers:
       Gloria, hosanna in excelsis!
       Gloria, hosanna in excelsis!

Words: G.R. Woodward (1848–1934)
Melody: 'Branche de l'Official' from Thoinot Arbeau's
'Orchésographie' (1588)

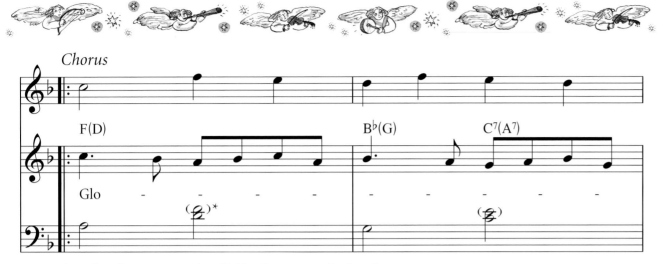

Chorus

*Bracketed notes are optional if the descant part is played.

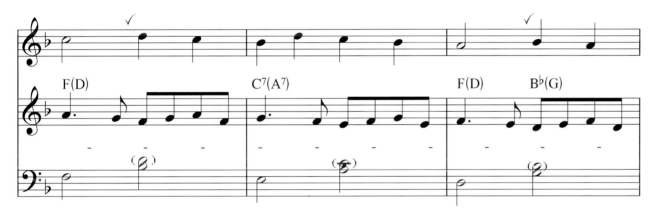

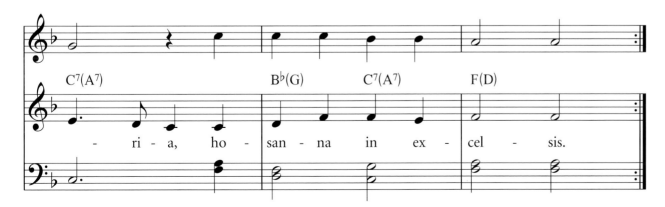

Tambour (tapped lightly through verse)

The part for melody instruments will work well on metallophone or glockenspiel.

The guitar chords in the chorus do not harmonize with the piano accompaniment.

God rest you merry, gentlemen

1 God rest you merry, gentlemen,
  Let nothing you dismay,
  For Jesus Christ our Saviour
  Was born upon this day
  To save us all from Satan's power
  When we were gone astray:
      O tidings of comfort and joy,
      Comfort and joy,
      O tidings of comfort and joy.

2 In Bethlehem in Jewry
  This blessèd babe was born,
  And laid upon a manger
  Upon this blessèd morn;
  The which his mother Mary
  Nothing did take in scorn:
      O tidings of comfort and joy…

3 From God our heavenly Father
  A blessèd angel came,
  And unto certain shepherds
  Brought tidings of the same,
  How that in Bethlehem was born
  The Son of God by name:
      O tidings of comfort and joy…

4 'Fear not', then said the angel,
  'Let nothing you affright.
  This day is born a Saviour,
  Of virtue, power and might;
  So frequently to vanquish all
  The friends of Satan quite':
      O tidings of comfort and joy…

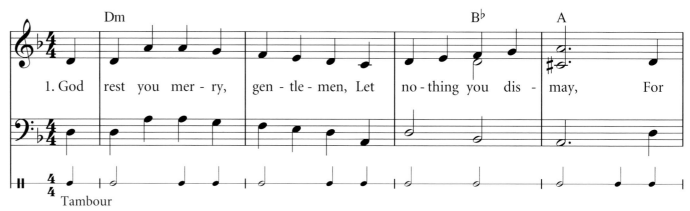

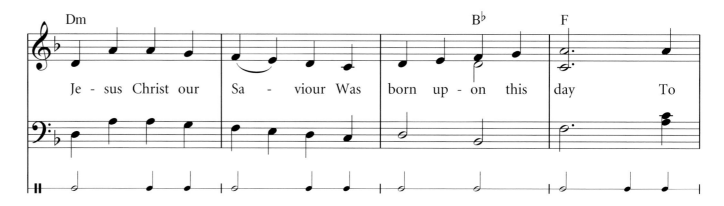

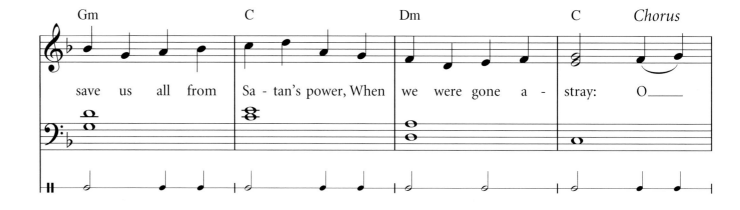

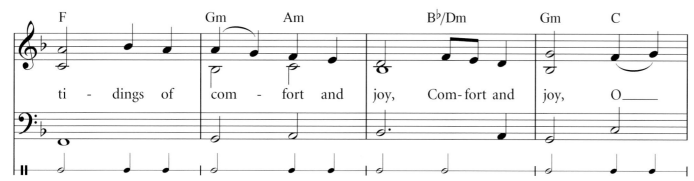

ti - dings of com - fort and joy, Com-fort and joy, O____

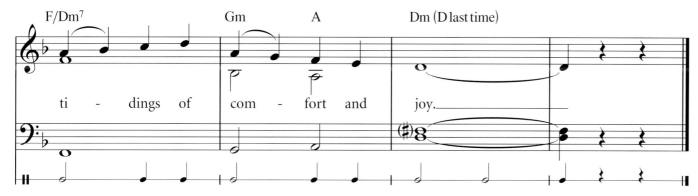

ti - dings of com - fort and joy.____

Melody instruments or tuned percussion (D F G A C′ D′ E′ F′ G′ A′)

5 The shepherds, at those tidings,
   Rejoicèd much in mind
   And left their flocks a-feeding
   In tempest, storm and wind,
   And went to Bethlehem straightway
   This blessèd babe to find:
       O tidings of comfort and joy…

6 And when they came to Bethlehem,
   Where our sweet Saviour lay,
   They found him in a manger,
   Where oxen feed on hay;
   His mother Mary kneeling,
   Unto the Lord did pray:
       O tidings of comfort and joy…

7 Now to the Lord sing praises,
   All you within this place,
   And with true love and brotherhood
   Each other now embrace;
   This holy tide of Christmas
   All others doth deface:
       O tidings of comfort and joy…

Words and melody: traditional English

Good Christian men, rejoice

1 Good Christian men, rejoice
   With heart and soul and voice;
   Give ye heed to what we say:
   Jesus Christ is born today!
   Ox and ass before him bow,
   And he is in the manger now.
       Christ is born today!
       Christ is born today!

2 Good Christian men, rejoice
   With heart and soul and voice;
   Now ye hear of endless bliss:
   Jesus Christ was born for this!
   Opens now the heavenly door
   And man is blessed for evermore.
       Christ was born for this!
       Christ was born for this!

3 Good Christian men, rejoice
   With heart and soul and voice;
   Now ye need not fear the grave:
   Jesus Christ was born to save!
   Calls you one and calls you all
   To gain his everlasting hall.
       Christ was born to save!
       Christ was born to save!

Words: J.M. Neale (1818–66)
Melody: 14th century German carol

In dulci jubilo

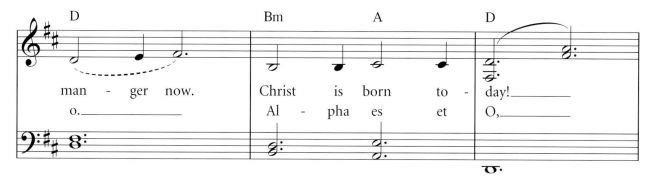

man - ger now.
o.
Christ is born to - day!
Al - pha es et O,

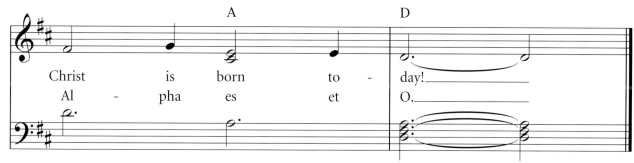

Christ is born to - day!
Al - pha es et O.

Tuned percussion (A, D E F♯ A D′ E′)

Indian bells

1 In dulci jubilo
   Let us our homage show;
   Our heart's joy reclineth
   In praesepio,
   And like a bright star shineth
   Matris in gremio.
      Alpha es et O,
      Alpha es et O.

2 O Jesu parvule!
   My heart is sore for thee!
   Hear me, I beseech thee,
   O puer optime!
   My prayer let it reach thee,
   O princeps gloriae!
      Trahe me post te!
      Trahe me post te!

3 Ubi sunt gaudia,
   If that they be not there?
   There are angels singing
   Nova cantica,
   There the bells are ringing
   In Regis curia:
      O that we were there!
      O that we were there!

Words: translated by R.L. de Pearsall (1795–1856)

Good King Wenceslas

1 Good King Wenceslas looked out
  On the feast of Stephen,
  When the snow lay round about,
  Deep and crisp and even.
  Brightly shone the moon that night,
  Though the frost was cruel,
  When a poor man came in sight,
  Gath'ring winter fuel.

2 'Hither, page, and stand by me,
  If thou knowest it, telling.
  Yonder peasant, who is he?
  Where and what his dwelling?'
  'Sire, he lives a good league hence,
  Underneath the mountain,
  Right against the forest fence
  By St Agnes fountain.'

3 'Bring me flesh and bring me wine,
  Bring me pine logs hither.
  Thou and I will see him dine,
  When we bear them thither.'
  Page and monarch, forth they went,
  Forth they went together;
  Through the rude wind's wild lament
  And the bitter weather.

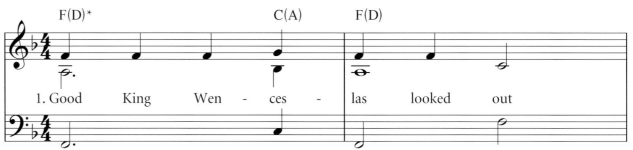

*Capo at third fret

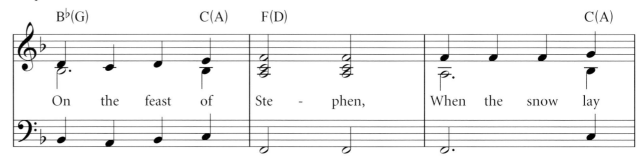

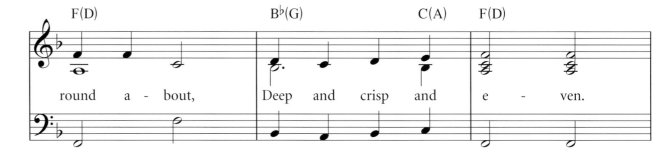

cru - el,   When a poor man   came in sight

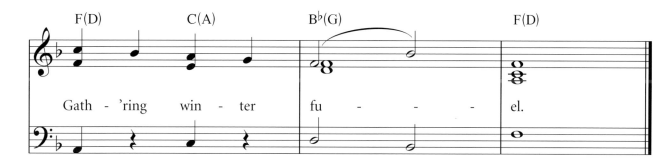

Gath - 'ring   win - ter   fu - - - el.

4 'Sire, the night is darker now,
   And the wind blows stronger.
   Fails my heart, I know not how,
   I can go no longer.'
   'Mark my footsteps, good my page,
   Tread thou in them boldly.
   Thou shalt find the winter's rage
   Freeze thy blood less coldly.'

5 In his master's steps he trod,
   Where the snow lay dinted.
   Heat was in the very sod,
   Which the saint had printed.
   Therefore, Christian men, be sure,
   Wealth or rank possessing,
   You who now will bless the poor
   Shall yourselves find blessing.

Words: J.M. Neale (1818–66)
Melody: 13th century spring song, 'Tempus adest
floridum', from 'Piae cantiones'

Easy recorders, tuned percussion (F A B♭ C′ D′ E′ F′)

Tambour, vv. 1, 3, 5

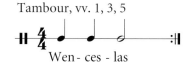

Wen - ces - las

Triangle, vv. 2 and 4

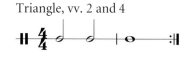

Hark! the herald angels sing

1 Hark! the herald angels sing
Glory to the new-born King;
Peace on earth and mercy mild,
God and sinners reconciled:
Joyful all ye nations rise,
Join the triumph of the skies,
With the angelic host proclaim:
Christ is born in Bethlehem.
   Hark! the herald angels sing
   Glory to the new-born King.

2 Christ, by highest heaven adored,
Christ, the everlasting Lord,
Late in time behold him come,
Offspring of a virgin's womb:
Veiled in flesh the Godhead see,
Hail the incarnate Deity!
Pleased as Man with man to dwell,
Jesus, our Emmanuel.
   Hark! the herald angels sing
   Glory to the new-born King.

3 Hail, the heaven-born Prince of Peace!
Hail the Sun of Righteousness!
Light and life to all he brings,
Risen with healing in his wings.
Mild he lays his glory by,
Born that man no more may die,
Born to raise the sons of earth,
Born to give them second birth.
   Hark! the herald angels sing
   Glory to the new-born King.

Words: Charles Wesley (1707–88)
Music: F. Mendelssohn-Bartholdy (1809–47)

Joy - ful all ye na - tions rise,___ Join the tri - umph of the skies,___
C(A) F(D) C(A) F(D) C(A) C(A) F(D) C(A) F(D) C(A)

Joy - ful all ye na - tions rise,___ Join the tri - umph of the skies,___

With th'an - ge - lic host pro - claim, Christ is born in Beth - le - hem:
B♭(G) Cm(Am) Gm(Em) D(B) Gm(Em) C(A) F(D) C(A) F(D)

With th'an - ge - lic host pro - claim, Christ is___ born in Beth - le - hem:

Hark! the he - rald an - gels sing Glo - ry to the new - born King.
B♭(G) Cm(Am) Gm(Em) D(B) Gm(Em) C(A) F(D) C(A) F(D)

Hark! the he - rald an - gels sing Glo - ry___ to the new - born King.

23

Here we come a-wassailing

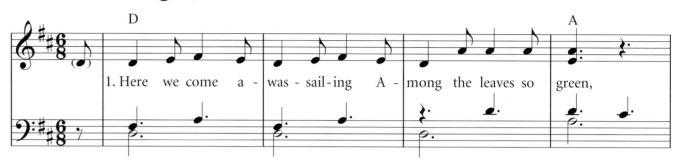

1. Here we come a-wassailing
   Among the leaves so green,
   Here we come a-wandering
   So fair to be seen.
   Love and joy come to you,
   And to you your wassail too,
   And God bless you and send you
       a happy New Year,
   And God send you a happy New Year.

2. Our wassail cup is made
   Of the rosemary tree,
   And so is your beer
   Of the best barley.
       Love and joy come to you…

3. Good Master and good Mistress,
   As you sit by the fire,
   Pray think of us poor children
   Who are wandering in the mire.
       Love and joy come to you…

Lyrics under staff: 1. Here we come a-was-sail-ing A-mong the leaves so green,
Here we come a-wan-der-ing So fair to be seen.

Verse: Tuned percussion (A D′ E′ F♯′ A′)

Chorus: Melody instruments (easy part stems down)

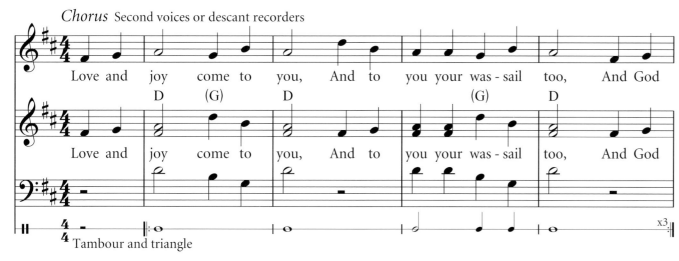

Chorus Second voices or descant recorders

Love and joy come to you, And to you your was-sail too, And God

D (G) D (G) D

Love and joy come to you, And to you your was-sail too, And God

Tambour and triangle

x3

4 Bring us out a table,
   And spread it with a cloth;
   Bring us out a mouldy cheese
   And some of your Christmas loaf.
      Love and joy…

5 God bless the Master of this house,
   Likewise the Mistress too,
   And all the little children
   That round the table go.
      Love and joy…

Words and melody: traditional English

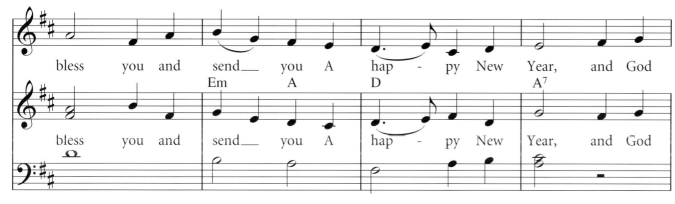

bless you and send___ you A hap - py New Year, and God

Em A D A⁷

bless you and send___ you A hap - py New Year, and God

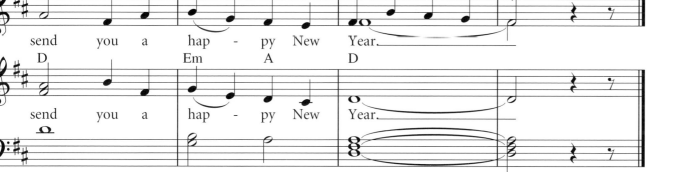

send you a hap - py New Year.___

D Em A D

send you a hap - py New Year.___

25

I saw three ships

1 I saw three ships come sailing in
   On Christmas Day, On Christmas Day,
   I saw three ships come sailing in
   On Christmas Day in the morning.

2 And what was in those ships all three?
   On Christmas Day, on Christmas Day…

3 Our Saviour Christ and his lady,
   On Christmas Day, on Christmas Day…

4 Pray, whither sailed those ships all three?
   On Christmas Day, on Christmas Day…

5 Oh, they sailed into Bethlehem
   On Christmas Day, on Christmas Day…

6 And all the bells on earth shall ring
   On Christmas Day, on Christmas Day…

7 And all the angels in heaven shall sing
   On Christmas Day, on Christmas Day…

Words and melodies: traditional English

Second tune
Descant recorders

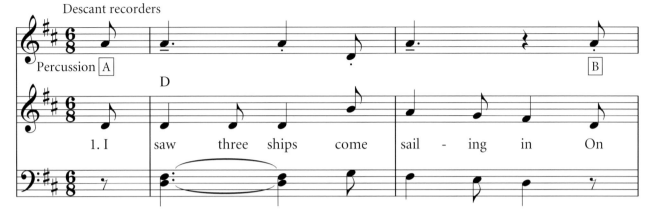

Percussion A   B

1. I saw three ships come sail - ing in On

Christ - mas Day, on Christ - mas Day, I saw three ships come

sail - ing in On Christ - mas Day in the morn - ing.

First tune: choose contrasting instruments to play these two rhythms, and vary the combination between verses.

Bells, tambourine or triangle

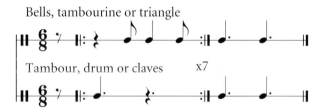

Tambour, drum or claves   x7

Tuned percussion (2 players – C/C′)   x4

Tuned percussion or tenors (F C′ F′)

Second tune: choose three different sounds, eg drum, triangle, Indian bells, and play the rhythm of the recorder part at A B and C. Play together at B + C.

27

In the bleak midwinter

1 In the bleak midwinter
   Frosty wind made moan;
   Earth stood hard as iron,
   Water like a stone;
   Snow had fallen, snow on snow,
   Snow on snow,
   In the bleak midwinter,
   Long ago.

2 Our God, heaven cannot hold him
   Nor earth sustain;
   Heaven and earth shall flee away
   When he comes to reign:
   In the bleak midwinter
   A stable-place sufficed
   The Lord God almighty,
   Jesus Christ.

3 What can I give him,
   Poor as I am?
   If I were a shepherd
   I would bring a lamb;
   If I were a wise man
   I would do my part;
   Yet what I can, I give him –
   Give my heart.

Words: Christina Rossetti (1830–94)
Melody: Gustav Holst (1874–1934)

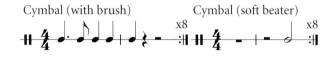

It came upon the midnight clear

1 It came upon the midnight clear,
That glorious song of old,
From angels bending near the earth
To touch their harps of gold:
'Peace on the earth, goodwill to men,
From heaven's all-gracious King!'
The world in solemn stillness lay
To hear the angels sing.

2 Yet with the woes of sin and strife
The world has suffered long;
Beneath the angel-strain have rolled
Two thousand years of wrong;
And man, at war with man, hears not
The love-song which they bring;
O hush the noise, ye men of strife,
And hear the angels sing.

3 For lo! the days are hastening on,
By prophet-bards foretold,
When, with the ever-circling years,
Comes round the age of gold;
When peace shall over all the earth
Its ancient splendours fling,
And the whole world give back the song
Which now the angels sing.

Words: E.H. Sears (1810–76)
Melody: traditional English melody adapted by Arthur Sullivan
(1842–1900)

Joseph dearest, Joseph mine

Mary:

1 Joseph dearest, Joseph mine,
 Help me cradle the child divine;
 God reward thee and all that's thine
 In paradise,
  so prays the mother Mary.

 He came among us at Christmastide,
 At Christmastide, in Bethlehem;
 Men shall bring him from far and wide
 Love's diadem:
  Jesus, Jesus,
 Lo, he comes, and loves, and saves,
  and frees us!

Joseph:

2 Gladly, dear one, lady mine,
 Help I cradle this child of thine;
 God's own light on us both shall shine
 In paradise,
  as prays the mother Mary.

Servants from the inn:

3 Peace to all that have goodwill!
 God, who heaven and earth doth fill,
 Comes to turn us away from ill,
 And lies so still
  within the crib of Mary.

Words: translated by Percy Dearmer (1867–1936)
Melody: 15th century German carol
Arrangement: J.B.

Christ - mas - tide, _____ (Hum)

came a-mong us at Christ-mas-tide, At Christ-mas-tide, In Beth-le-hem;

Men shall bring him from far and wide Love's di - a - dem: Je - sus,

Men shall bring him from far and wide Love's di - a - dem: Je - sus,

Je - sus, *ah.* _____

Je - sus, Lo, he comes, and loves, and saves, and frees us!

Solo voices may take the parts of Mary and Joseph, and of servants from the inn. A group of voices might sing the second voice part.

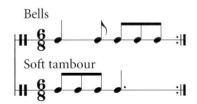

Bells

Soft tambour

31

Little Jesus, sweetly sleep

1 Little Jesus, sweetly sleep, do not stir;
We will lend a coat of fur.
We will rock you, rock you, rock you,
We will rock you, rock you, rock you:
See the fur to keep you warm,
Snugly round your tiny form.

2 Mary's little baby, sleep, sweetly sleep,
Sleep in comfort, slumber deep.
We will rock you, rock you, rock you,
We will rock you, rock you, rock you:
We will serve you all we can,
Darling, darling little man.

Words: translated by Percy Dearmer (1867–1936)
Melody: traditional Czech carol collected by Martin Shaw (1875–1958)

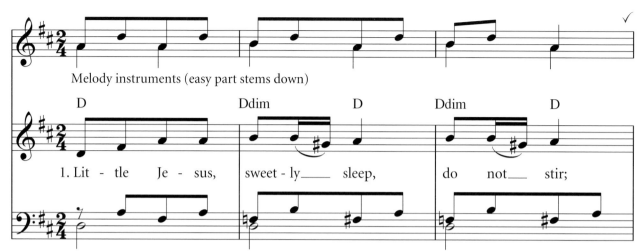

• © 2008 A&C Black Publishers Ltd

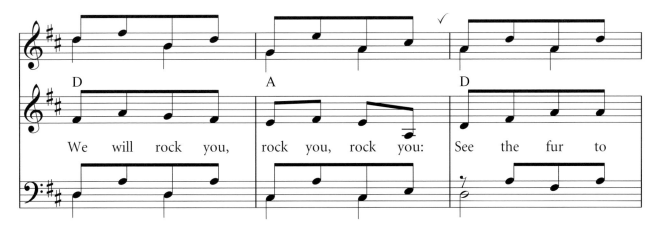

D   A   D

We will rock you, rock you, rock you: See the fur to

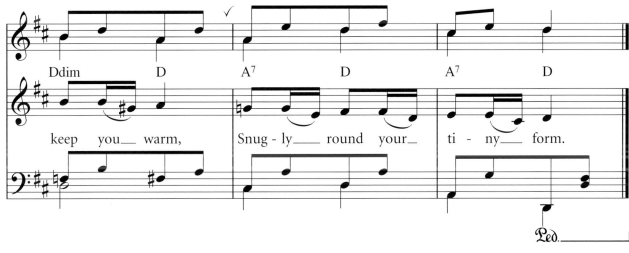

Ddim   D   A⁷   D   A⁷   D

keep you__ warm,   Snug - ly__ round your__ ti - ny__ form.

Ped._____

Tuned percussion

This part will work well on alto or bass metallophone, or lower sounding chime bars (A, B, D).

Untuned percussion

Cymbal with brush, maracas or Indian bells

Tambour with soft beater, tambourine or drum

33

Lully, lulla

Lully, lulla, thou little tiny child,
By by, lully, lullay.

1 O sisters too,
   How may we do
   For to preserve this day
   This poor youngling,
   For whom we do sing,
   By by, lully lullay?
       Lully, lulla…

2 Herod, the King,
   In his raging,
   Chargèd he hath this day
   His men of might,
   In his own sight,
   All young children to slay.
       Lully, lulla…

3 That woe is me,
   Poor child for thee!
   And ever morn and day,
   For thy parting
   Neither say nor sing
   By by, lully lullay!
       Lully, lulla…

*Words: from the Coventry Tailors' and Shearmen's pageant
(15th century)*
Melody: modern version of a tune of 1591

For to pre - serve this day This poor young - ling, For

Em   Am   B⁷   Em   D   Em   B   Em

For to pre - serve this___ day This poor young - ling, For

D. C. al Fine

whom we do sing, By by, lul - ly lul - lay?

D   Em   B   Em   Am   B⁷   E

whom we do sing, By by, lul - ly lul - lay?

Recorders

Descant recorders can play the melody; tenors can play the part given below;
trebles can play the second voice part – play G instead of E (small notes).

Fine

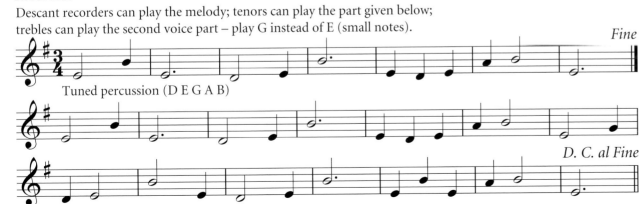

Tuned percussion (D E G A B)

D. C. al Fine

Nowell, sing Nowell

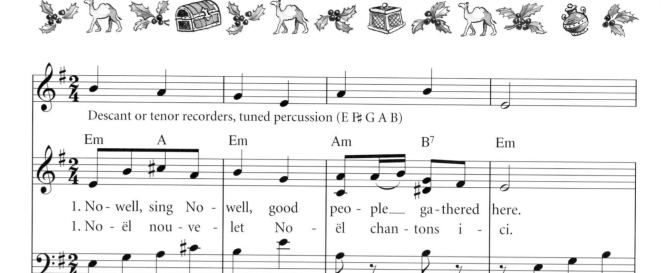

1 Nowell, sing Nowell, good people gathered here.
Offer thanks, ye faithful, to the news give ear.
Sing we Nowell, a new King born today.
    Nowell, sing Nowell,
    Good people gathered here.

2 Unto humble shepherds came the angel near;
'Hence', said he, 'to Bethlem, be ye of good cheer.
Seek there the Lamb of God, love's own pure ray.'
    Nowell, sing Nowell…

3 When to Bethlehem they came in lowly fear,
Found they gentle Mary with her son so dear.
Heaven's mighty Lord all cradled in the hay,
    Nowell, sing Nowell…

4 Eastern sages seek him, in the darkness drear
By a star illumined shining forth so clear,
Guiding them to Bethlem far away.
    Nowell, sing Nowell…

5 Now doth our Saviour Jesus Christ appear,
Bringing salvation, promised many a year,
By his redeeming blood this happy day.
    Nowell, sing Nowell…

Descant or tenor recorders, tuned percussion (E F♯ G A B)

1. No - well, sing No - well, good peo - ple__ ga - thered here.
1. No - ël nou - ve - let No - ël chan - tons i - ci.

Of - fer thanks, ye faith - ful, to the__ news give ear.
Dé - vo - tes__ gens, cri - ons à__ Dieu mer - ci!

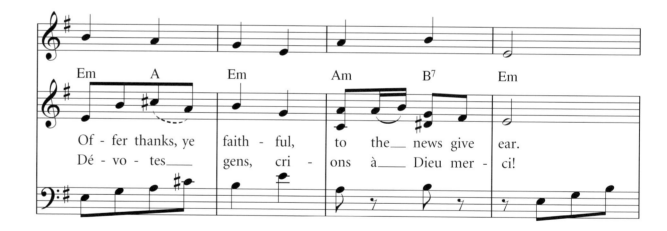

Noël nouvelet

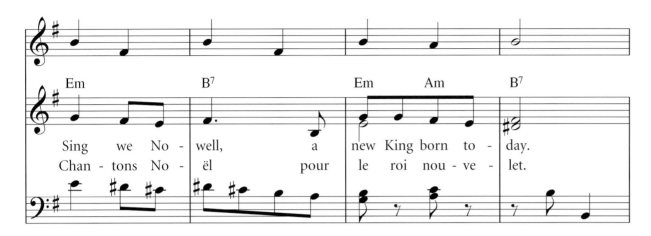

Sing we No - well, a new King born to - day.
Chan - tons No - ël pour le roi nou - ve - let.

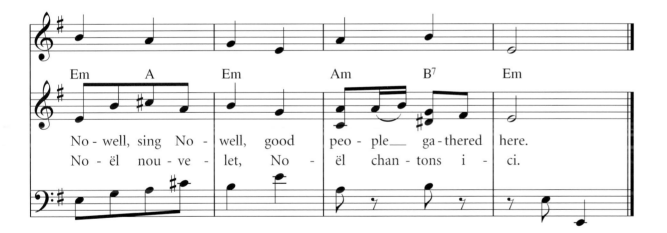

No - well, sing No - well, good peo - ple ga - thered here.
No - ël nou - ve - let, No - ël chan - tons i - ci.

1 Noël nouvelet, Noël chantons ici.
Dévotes gens, crions à Dieu merci!
Chantons Noël pour le roi nouvelet.
Noël nouvelet, Noël chantons ici.

2 L'ange disait: pasteurs, partez d'ici
L'âme en repos et le coeur réjoui;
En Bethléem trouverez l'agnelet.
Noël nouvelet, Noël chantons ici.

3 En Bethléem, étant tous réunis,
Trouvent l'enfant, Joseph, Marie aussi.
La crèche était au lieu d'un bercelet.
Noël nouvelet, Noël chantons ici.

4 Bientôt les rois, par l'ëtoile éclaircis
De l'orient dont ils étaient sortis
A Bethléem vinrent un matinet.
Noël nouvelet, Noël chantons ici.

5 Voici mon Dieu, mon Sauveur Jésus-Christ,
Par qui sera le prodige accompli
De nous sauver par son sang vermeillet!
Noël nouvelet, Noël chantons ici.

Words: 'Noël nouvelet', translated by John Rutter (b. 1945)
Melody: traditional French carol

Untuned percussion (vary between verses)
Tambourine, bells or triangle

Drum, tambour or bongos

O come, all ye faithful

1 O come, all ye faithful,
   Joyful and triumphant,
   O come ye, O come ye to Bethlehem;
   Come and behold him,
   Born the King of angels.
      O come let us adore him,
      O come let us adore him,
      O come let us adore him,
      Christ the Lord!

2 God of God,
   Light of light,
   Lo! He abhors not the Virgin's womb;
   Very God,
   Begotten not created.
      O come let us adore him…

3 Sing, choirs of angels,
   Sing in exultation,
   Sing, all ye citizens of heaven above:
   Glory to God
   In the highest.
      O come let us adore him…

4 Yea, Lord, we greet thee,
   Born this happy morning,
   Jesu, to thee be glory given;
   Word of the Father,
   Now in flesh appearing:
      O come let us adore him…

Words: translated from the Latin by F. Oakeley (1802–80)
Melody: 'Adeste Fideles', 18th century Latin hymn

*Capo at third fret

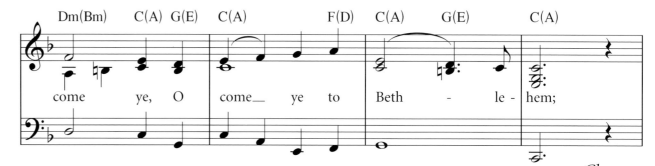

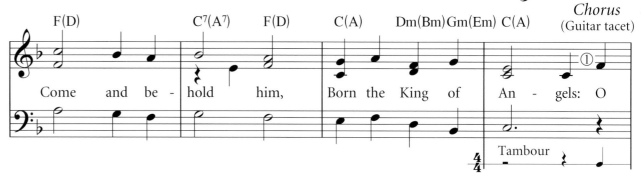

Verse percussion

Jingles or Indian bells

Drum or tambour

Recorder ensemble

Chorus – parts ① ② ③. Let everyone try each line and give them an opportunity to listen to the different combinations when deciding on the variations for each verse, considering a build-up to the climax of the last chorus. Other melody instruments can use the parts in the same way.

O little town of Bethlehem

1 O little town of Bethlehem,
   How still we see thee lie!
   Above thy deep and dreamless sleep
   The silent stars go by.
   Yet in thy dark streets shineth
   The everlasting light;
   The hopes and fears of all the years
   Are met in thee tonight.

2 O morning stars, together
   Proclaim the holy birth,
   And praises sing to God the King,
   And peace to men on earth;
   For Christ is born of Mary;
   And, gathered all above,
   While mortals sleep the angels keep
   Their watch of wondering love.

3 How silently, how silently
   The wondrous gift is given!
   So God imparts to human hearts
   The blessings of his heaven.
   No ear may hear his coming,
   But in this world of sin
   Where meek souls will receive him, still
   The dear Christ enters in.

Second voices, melody instruments

*Capo at third fret

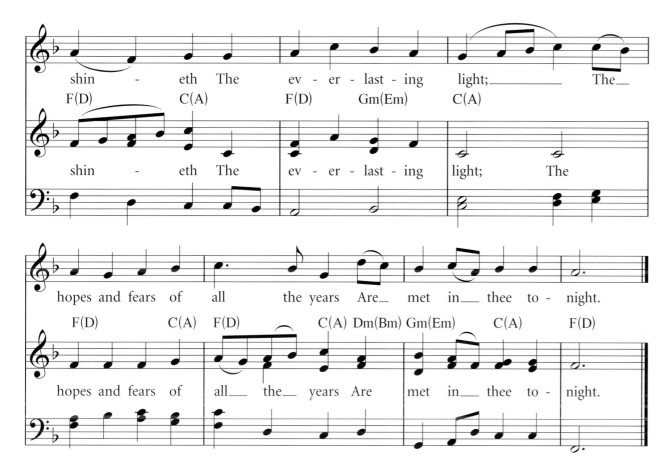

shin - eth The ev - er - last - ing light;_____ The_

F(D)   C(A)   F(D)   Gm(Em)   C(A)

shin - eth The ev - er - last - ing light; The

hopes and fears of all the years Are_ met in_ thee to - night.

F(D)   C(A) F(D)   C(A) Dm(Bm) Gm(Em)   C(A)   F(D)

hopes and fears of all_ the_ years Are met in_ thee to - night.

4 Where children pure and happy
   Pray to the blessèd Child,
   Where misery cries out to thee,
   Son of the mother mild;
   Where charity stands watching
   And faith holds wide the door,
   The dark night wakes, the glory breaks,
   And Christmas comes once more.

5 O holy child of Bethlehem,
   Descend to us, we pray;
   Cast out our sin and enter in,
   Be born in us today.
   We hear the Christmas angels
   The great glad tidings tell:
   O come to us, abide with us,
   Our Lord Emmanuel.

Words: Bishop Philips Brooks (1835–93)
Melody: 'Forest Green', traditional English tune
adapted by R. Vaughan Williams (1872–1958)

Instrumentation
The melody line and two second parts can be played by a wide range of instruments including all the recorders (sopranino and treble can play the melody line if they play lower C one octave higher).

Recorders, tuned percussion (F G A C' D')

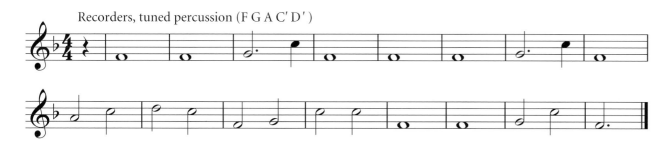

On Christmas night

1 On Christmas night all Christians sing
To hear the news the angels bring;
On Christmas night all Christians sing
To hear the news the angels bring:
   News of great joy, news of great mirth,
   News of our merciful King's birth.

2 Then why should men on earth be so sad
Since our Redeemer made us glad;
Then why should men on earth be so sad
Since our Redeemer made us glad,
   When from our sin he set us free,
   All for to gain our liberty?

3 All out of darkness we have light
Which made the angels sing this night;
All out of darkness we have light
Which made the angels sing this night:
   'Glory to God and peace to men,
   Now and for evermore, amen.'

Words and melody: traditional English,
collected by R. Vaughan Williams (1872–1958)

News of great joy,__ news of__ great mirth,

Percussion tacent

A

D   G   D   A   D

News of our mer - ci - ful__ King's birth.__

Instrumentation

Tuned percussion can play the guitar chord letter names (D G A).

① – Easier part for all melody instruments.
This can be repeated in bars 5–8.

② – Harder part for all melody instruments.
Play the parts separately, or together for a grand joyous effect.

Contrasting pairs of untuned percussion can play the rhythm of the words at ①, ② and ①+②.

43

Once in royal David's city

1 Once in royal David's city
Stood a lowly cattle shed,
Where a mother laid her baby
In a manger for his bed.
    Mary was that mother mild,
    Jesus Christ her little child.

2 He came down to earth from heaven,
Who is God and Lord of all,
And his shelter was a stable,
And his cradle was a stall.
    With the poor, and mean, and lowly,
    Lived on earth our Saviour holy.

3 For he is our childhood's pattern,
Day by day like us he grew.
He was little, weak and helpless,
Tears and smiles like us he knew.
    And he feeleth for our sadness,
    And he shareth in our gladness.

4 And our eyes at last shall see him
Through his own redeeming love.
For that child so dear and gentle
Is our Lord in heaven above.
    And he leads his children on
    To the place where he is gone.

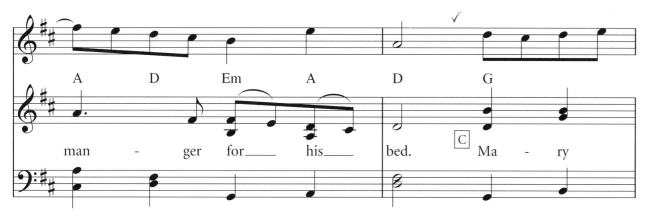

man - ger for his bed. [C] Ma - ry

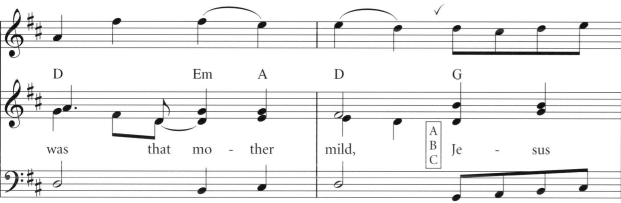

was that mo - ther mild, [A][B][C] Je - sus

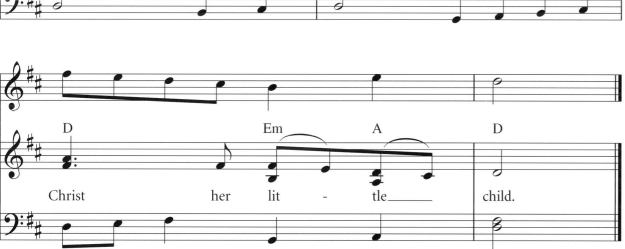

Christ her lit - tle child.

Untuned percussion
Play the rhythm of the words at
[A] on bells or triangles,
[B] on tambourine,
[C] on maracas or woodblock.
Play together at [A+B+C]

Words: Mrs C.F. Alexander (1818–95)
Melody: 'Irby' by H.J. Gauntlett (1805–76)

See, amid the winter's snow

1 See, amid the winter's snow,
  Born for us on earth below;
  See, the tender Lamb appears,
  Promised from eternal years:
      Hail, thou ever-blessèd morn;
      Hail, redemption's happy dawn;
      Sing through all Jerusalem,
      Christ is born in Bethlehem.

2 Lo, within a manger lies
  He who built the starry skies;
  He who, throned in height sublime,
  Sits amid the cherubim:
      Hail, thou ever-blessèd morn…

3 Say, ye holy shepherds, say
  What your joyful news today;
  Wherefore have ye left your sheep
  On the lonely mountain steep?
      Hail, thou ever-blessèd morn…

4 'As we watched at dead of night,
  Lo, we saw a wondrous light;
  Angels singing "Peace on earth"
  Told us of the Saviour's birth':
      Hail, thou ever-blessèd morn…

Words: E. Caswall (1814–78)
Melody: John Goss (1800–80)

Chorus

Treble recorders

F(D)   C(A)

Hail, thou ev - er - bless - ed morn;

B

Hail, re-demp-tion's hap-py dawn; Sing through all Je-

F(D)   C(A)   C⁷(A⁷)   F(D)

B♭(G)   F(D)   B♭(G)   C(A) C⁷(A⁷) F(D)

-ru - sa - lem, Christ is born in Beth - le - hem.

Untuned percussion
Choose a variety of gentle-sounding instruments
to play the repeated rhythms [A] and [B]. Let them
play the rhythms singly or in combination.

Tambour or drum (soft beaters)
or cymbal with brush

47

Shepherds left their flocks a-straying

1 Shepherds left their flocks a-straying,
  God's command with joy obeying,
  When they heard the angel saying:
  'Christ is born in Bethlehem.'

2 Wise men came from far, and saw him,
  Knelt in homage to adore him,
  Precious gifts they laid before him:
  Gold and frankincense and myrrh.

3 Let us now in every nation
  Sing his praise with exultation.
  All the world shall find salvation
  In the birth of Mary's son.

Words: Imogen Holst (1907–84)
Melody: 'Quem Pastores', 14th century German melody

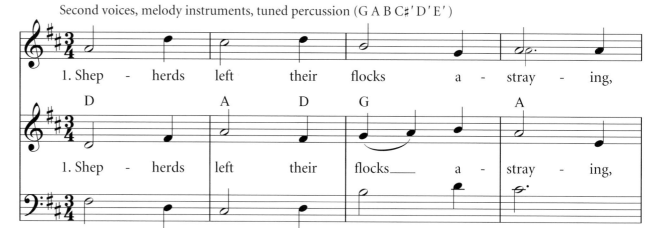

Second voices, melody instruments, tuned percussion (G A B C♯′ D′ E′)

1. Shep - herds left their flocks a - stray - ing,

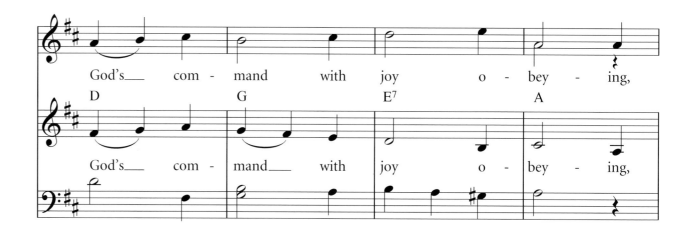

God's___ com - mand with joy o - bey - ing,

Untuned percussion
Choose one pair of instruments for each verse:

Claves, tambour or Indian bells

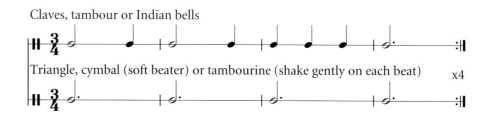

Triangle, cymbal (soft beater) or tambourine (shake gently on each beat) x4

When ___ they heard the an - gel say - ing:

D

When they heard the an - gel say - ing:

'Christ is born ___ in Beth - le - hem.'

G   C   D   G   A⁷   D

'Christ is born ___ in Beth - le - hem.'

Tuned percussion (E F♯ G A B / G, A, D E G)
Play part 2 alone or together with part 1

① ②

49

Silent night

1 Silent night, holy night!
All is calm, all is bright
Round yon virgin mother and child.
Holy infant so tender and mild,
Sleep in heavenly peace,
Sleep in heavenly peace.

2 Silent night, holy night!
Shepherds quake at the sight:
Glories stream from heaven afar,
Heavenly hosts sing: Alleluia,
Christ the Saviour is born!
Christ the Saviour is born!

3 Silent night, holy night!
Son of God, love's pure light,
Radiance beams from thy holy face
With the dawn of redeeming grace,
Jesus, Lord at thy birth,
Jesus, Lord at thy birth.

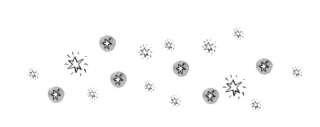

Stille Nacht

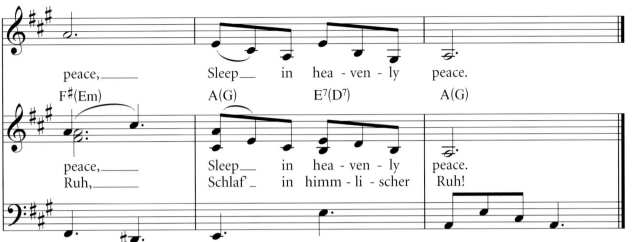

Second voice part: this can be transposed up an octave and sung or played by treble recorder or flute.

Tuned percussion (eg alto or bass metallophone)

Untuned percussion
Choose a selection of instruments to play each two-bar phrase of the melody rhythm very softly. For example:

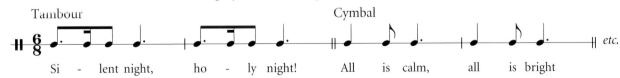

Alternatively choose two soft-sounding instruments to play this rhythm:

1 Stille Nacht, heilige Nacht!
Alles schläft, einsam wacht
Nur das traute, hochheilige Paar.
Holder Knabe im lockigen Haar,
Schlaf' in himmlischer Ruh,
Schalf' in himmlischer Ruh!

2 Stille Nacht, heilige Nacht!
Hirten erst kundegemacht,
Durch der Engel Halleluja
Tönt es laut von fern und nah:
Christ, der Retter, ist da,
Christ, der Retter, ist da!

3 Stille Nacht, heilige Nacht!
Gottes Sohn, O wie lacht
Lieb' aus deinem göttlichen Mund,
Da uns schägt die rettende Stund,
Christ in deiner Geburt,
Christ, in deiner Geburt!

Words: Joseph Mohr (1792–1848), translator anon.
Melody: Franz Gruber (1787–1863)

Sing aloud on this day

1 Sing aloud on this day!
  Children all raise the lay.
  Cheerfully we and they
  Hasten to adore thee,
  Sent from highest glory,
  For us born, born, born,
  For us born, born, born,
  For us born on this morn
  Of the Virgin Mary.

2 Now a child he is born,
  Swathing bands him adorn,
  Manger bed he'll not scorn.
  Ox and ass are near him;
  We as Lord revere him,
  And the vain, vain, vain,
  And the vain, vain, vain,
  And the vain powers of hell
  Spoiled of prey now fear him.

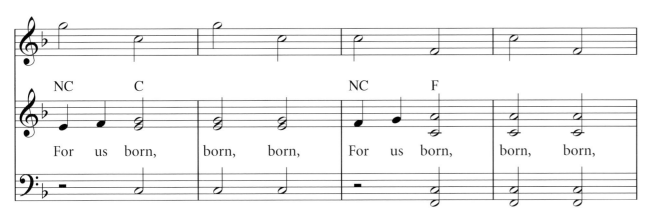

NC C   NC F

For us born, born, born, For us born, born, born,

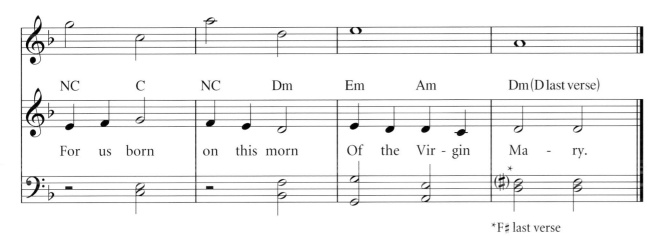

NC C NC Dm Em Am Dm (D last verse)

For us born on this morn Of the Vir - gin Ma - ry.

*F♯ last verse

3 From the far Orient
  Guiding star wise men sent;
  Him to seek their intent,
  Lord of all creation;
  Kneel in adoration.
  Gifts of gold, gold, gold,
  Gifts of gold, gold, gold,
  Gifts of gold, frankincense,
  Myrrh for their oblation.

4 All must join him to praise,
  Girls and boys voices raise
  On this day of all days;
  Angel voices ringing,
  Christmas tidings bringing.
  Join we all, all, all,
  Join we all, all, all,
  Join we all, Gloria
  In excelsis, singing.

Words: John A. Parkinson
Melody: old German melody from 'Piae Cantiones'

The first Nowell

1 The first Nowell the angel did say
   Was to certain poor shepherds in fields
       as they lay;
   In fields where they lay, keeping their sheep,
   On a cold winter's night that was so deep:
       Nowell, Nowell, Nowell, Nowell,
       Born is the King of Israel!

2 They lookèd up and saw a star
   Shining in the east, beyond them far.
   And to the earth it gave great light,
   And so it continued both day and night:
       Nowell, Nowell, Nowell, Nowell…

3 And by the light of that same star,
   Three wise men came from country far.
   To seek for a King was their intent,
   And to follow the star wheresoever it went:
       Nowell, Nowell, Nowell, Nowell…

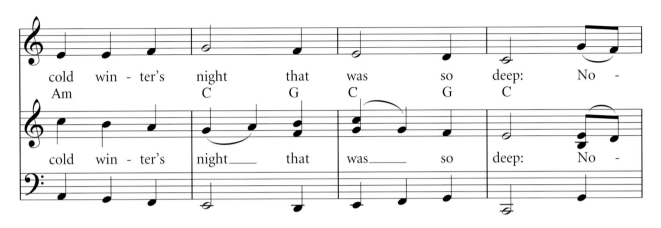

cold win-ter's night that was so deep: No-

Am   C   G   C   G   C

cold win-ter's night___ that was___ so deep: No-

- well___ No - well, No - well, No - well,

Am   G   F   C

- well___ No - well, No - well, No - well,

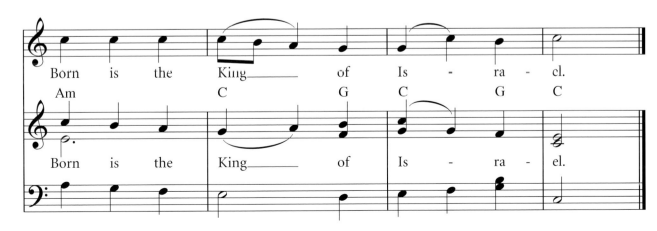

Born is the King___ of Is - ra - el.

Am   C   G   C   G   C

Born is the King___ of Is - ra - el.

4 This star drew nigh to the north-west;
   O'er Bethlehem it took its rest,
   And there it did both stop and stay
   Right over the place where Jesus lay:
      Nowell, Nowell, Nowell, Nowell…

5 Then entered in those wise men three,
   Fell reverently upon their knee,
   And offered there in his presence
   Both gold and myrrh and frankincense:
      Nowell, Nowell, Nowell, Nowell…

6 Then let us all with one accord
   Sing praises to our heavenly Lord,
   Who hath made heaven and earth of naught,
   And with his blood mankind hath bought:
      Nowell, Nowell, Nowell, Nowell…

Words and melody: traditional English

55

The holly and the ivy

1 The holly and the ivy,
  When they are both full grown,
  Of all the trees that are in the wood
  The holly bears the crown:
    O the rising of the sun
    And the running of the deer,
    The playing of the merry organ,
    Sweet singing in the choir.

2 The holly bears a blossom
  As white as any flower,
  And Mary bore sweet Jesus Christ
  To be our sweet Saviour:
    O the rising of the sun…

Chorus

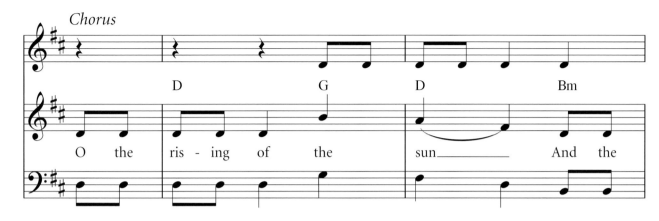

O the ris - ing of the sun_____ And the

run - ning of the deer, The___ play - ing of the

mer - ry or - gan, Sweet sing - ing in the choir.

3 The holly bears a berry
   As red as any blood,
   And Mary bore sweet Jesus Christ
   To do poor sinners good:
      O the rising of the sun…

4 The holly and the ivy,
   When they are both full grown,
   Of all the trees that are in the wood
   The holly bears the crown:
      O the rising of the sun…

Words and melody: traditional English,
collected by Cecil Sharp (1859–1924)

Unto us a boy is born!

1 Unto us a boy is born!
  King of all creation,
  Came he to a world forlorn,
  The Lord of every nation,
  The Lord of every nation.

2 Cradled in a stall was he
  With sleepy cows and asses;
  But the very beasts could see
  That he all men surpasses,
  That he all men surpasses.

3 Omega and Alpha he!
  Let the organ thunder,
  While the choir with peals of glee
  Doth rend the air asunder,
  Doth rend the air asunder.

Words: 'Puer nobis nascitur', translated by Geoffrey Shaw (1879–1943)
Melody: old German melody from 'Piae Cantiones'

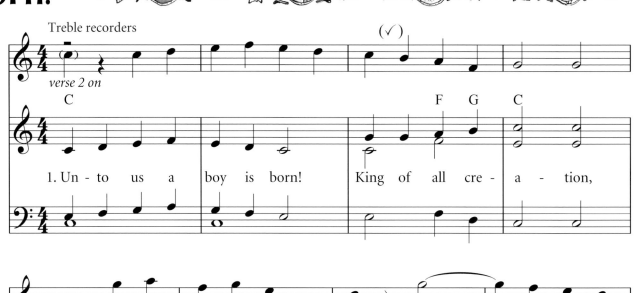

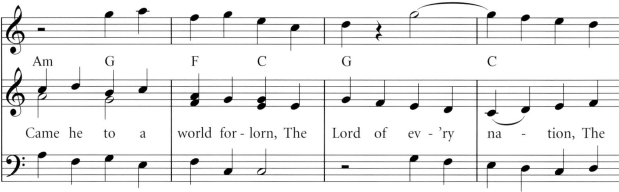

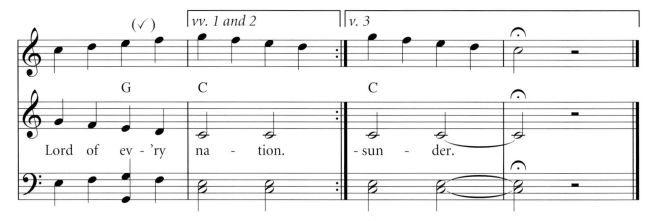

While shepherds watched

1 While shepherds watched their flocks by night,
All seated on the ground,
The angel of the Lord came down
And glory shone around.

2 'Fear not,' said he, for mighty dread
Had seized their troubled mind;
'Glad tidings of great joy I bring
To you and all mankind.

3 'To you in David's town this day
Is born of David's line
A Saviour, who is Christ the Lord,
And this shall be the sign:

4 'The heavenly babe you there shall find
To human view displayed,
All meanly wrapped in swathing bands,
And in a manger laid.'

5 Thus spake the seraph, and forthwith
Appeared a shining throng
Of angels praising God, who thus
Addressed their joyful song:

6 'All glory be to God on high,
And to the earth be peace,
Goodwill henceforth from heaven to men
Begin and never cease.'

Words: Nahum Tate (1652–1715)
Melody: 'Winchester Old' from 'Este's Psalter' (1592)

We three kings of Orient are

1 We three kings of Orient are;
   Bearing gifts we traverse afar,
   Field and fountain, moor and mountain,
   Following yonder star.
      O star of wonder, star of night,
      Star with royal beauty bright,
      Westward leading, still proceeding,
      Guide us to thy perfect light.

Melchior:

2 Born a king on Bethlehem's plain,
   Gold I bring to crown him again
   King for ever, ceasing never
   Over us all to reign.
      O star of wonder, star of night…

Caspar:

3 Frankincense to offer have I,
   Incense owns a Deity nigh.
   Prayer and praising, all men raising,
   Worship him, God most high.
      O star of wonder, star of night…

Balthazar:

4 Myrrh is mine; its bitter perfume
   Breathes a life of gathering gloom.
   Sorrowing, sighing, bleeding, dying,
   Sealed in the stone-cold tomb.
      O star of wonder, star of night…

5 Glorious now behold him arise,
   King, and God, and sacrifice!
   Heaven sings alleluia,
   Alleluia the earth replies
      O star of wonder, star of night…

Second voice, descant or treble recorders

star of won- der, star of night, Star with

star of won- der, star of night, Star with
F   B♭   F
F   F   B♭   F   F

roy- al beau- ty bright, West- ward lead- ing,
B♭   F   Dm   C
roy- al beau- ty bright, West- ward lead- ing,
F   B♭   F   D   C

still pro- ceed- ing, Guide us to thy per- fect light.
B♭   C   F   B♭   F
still pro- ceed- ing, Guide us to thy per- fect light.
B♭   C   F   F   B♭   F

Untuned percussion
Verse – use tambourine, triangle, bells or claves, either singly or together in this rhythm:

Chorus – bongos can improvise round the rhythm of the words.

Tambour and bell spray

Words and melody: J.H. Hopkins (1820-91)

61

What child is this?

1 What child is this, who, laid to rest
  On Mary's lap, is sleeping?
  Whom angels greet with anthems sweet,
  While shepherds watch are keeping?
      This, this is Christ the King,
      Whom shepherds worship and angels sing:
      Haste, haste to bring him praise,
      The babe, the son of Mary.

2 Why lies he in such mean estate,
  Where ox and ass are feeding?
  Come, have no fear, God's son is here,
  His love all loves exceeding.
      Nails, spear, shall pierce him through,
      The cross be borne for me, for you:
      Hail, hail, the Saviour comes,
      The babe, the son of Mary.

3 So bring him incense, gold and myrrh,
  All tongues and peoples own him.
  The King of Kings salvation brings,
  Let every heart enthrone him:
      Raise, raise your song on high
      While Mary sings a lullaby;
      Joy, joy, for Christ is born,
      The babe, the son of Mary.

Words: W. Chatterton Dix (1837–98)
Melody: 'Greensleeves', English traditional

Descant recorders

Tuned percussion (C D E F A)

F   C   Dm

This,   this___ is   Christ the   King,___Whom   shep - herds wor - ship and

Am   F   C

an - gels sing: Haste,   haste___ to   bring him praise,___ The

Dm   A   D

babe,___ the son___ of   Ma -   ry.

Tambour or drum with soft beater

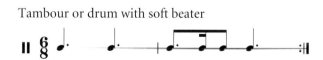

63

We wish you a merry Christmas

1 We wish you a merry Christmas,
  We wish you a merry Christmas,
  We wish you a merry Christmas,
  And a happy New Year.
    Good tidings we bring
    To you and your kin,
    We wish you a merry Christmas
    And a happy New Year.

2 Now bring us some figgy pudding…
    (three times)
  And bring some out here.
    Good tidings we bring…

3 And we won't go until we've got some…
    (three times)
  So bring some out here.
    Good tidings we bring…

Words and melody: English traditional

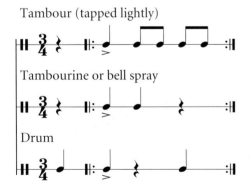